You Can Mak
The Best Hot Tub Ever!

By Becky Bee

Relax! Warm your Bones!
Get to Know the Sky!

Library of Congress Cataloging in Publication Data

Bee, Becky
YOU CAN MAKE THE BEST HOT TUB EVER! Relax! Warm Your
Bones! Get To Know The Sky!

Library of Congress Catalog Card Number: # available upon request

ISBN (paperback) 0-9659082-1-6

Illustrations by Becky Bee
Book Design & Layout by Becky Bee & Alex McMillan
Photographs that are not identified were taken by Becky Bee
Distributed by Chelsea Green 800-639-4099

Ordering Information

For copies of this book send your address and:
(within the US or Canada) US$14.95 this includes shipping costs. Add US$11.95
for each additional book
(outside the US or Canada) US$19.95 this includes shipping costs. Add US$17.95
for each additional book
to: **GROUNDWORKS** P.O. Box 381, Murphy, OR 97533, U.S.A.
cob@beckybee.net
www.beckybee.net
Contact us for bulk ordering details.

In Australasia contact:
Alex McMillan PO Box 488, Thames, New Zealand
her email is on the webpage

Thank you!

A special thanks to everyone who has ever built a hot tub with me. And to all of you who helped with the photos and the creation of this booklet. Warm blessings. Becky Bee

Be forwarned!

Becky and all the people who have contributed to this booklet do not assume responsibility for the mental and physical health and happiness resulting from the use of the information in this booklet. It is all yours!

Neither do we assume responsibility for damages, losses or injuries that may arise from the use of the information in this booklet. Every project and situation is unique. Fire and water can be hazardous so use good judgement and common sense. Please take good care of yourself, each other and our Mother Earth.

After years of smoky outdoor baths and burnt elbows and knees, Becky Bee discovered cob and made the bath of her dreams! So many friends wanted one that she decided to make this book so even friends she hasn't met can have the pleasure of making and owning the best hot tub ever!

Becky Bee also wrote the classic, _"The Cob Builders Handbook, You Can Hand-Sculpt Your Own Home"_ which is a detailed description on how to make a cob building.

CONTENTS

INTRODUCTION 1

PLANNING YOUR HOT TUB 5

  Things to consider 5

    The tub itself 6

      Horse troughs 8

      Round hot tubs 9

      Enameled steel baths 10

      Cast iron tubs 11

      Wooden tubs 11

    Choose a naturally dry place for your tub or create one. 12

    Where is the bath water coming from? 12

    Drain the tub to somewhere sensible. 12

    How will the tub sit on the slope of the land? 13

    Where does the firewood shed/bath house sit in relation to the tub? 13

    What do you want to look at when you're at repose in the tub? 14

    Which way does the wind blow? 14

    Privacy is nice while bathing. 14

    Get the tub, materials, water and firewood to the site. 14

    Design the area around the tub too. 15

MATERIALS LIST FOR YOUR HOT TUB: 16

    for a basic tub: 16

    for a more "sophisticated" tub: 16

  Tools: 17

OK, TIME TO MAKE THE TUB! 18

  Main diagram of wood-fired hot tub 19

The foundation 20
    The whole idea 20
    Starting your foundation 22
    Height of the tub off the ground 25
    The rest of the tub's foundation 27
    Foundation for the drain end of tub 28
    Foundation for the stove pipe 29
    A bump on the firebox floor 30
Cob 31
    Making test bricks 33
    Making cob 34
    Building with cob 35
The stove pipe 37
Decorating and protecting the cob from the weather 40
    Protecting the cob 41
    Protecting the cob with plaster 43
    Beautifying your bathing area 44
THE ART OF USING A WOOD FIRED TUB! 46
    Firing up the tub 47
    Hot seat! 48
    Sharing the bath with friends 49
ENJOY YOURSELF!

INTRODUCTION

Unless you have had an outdoor wood fired bath, there is no way your imagination can see how absolutely divine it is! It is more like a temple than a bath. It is the reclaiming of an old ritual, bringing together the elements in a light natural way,

Earth   Sculpting the mud and the physicalness of being outdoors in your birthday suit
            is a grounding experience.

Water   The sounds of water, and the body floating, lets the emotions flow.

Fire   Tending the magic of fire lets your creativity well up with the dream like state
           of fire watching.

Air   Breathing the breeze and watching the smoke drift, gives you the relaxation
          time for intuitive thoughts to come to the surface.

All in all it's a simple way to get closer to yourself.

Armed with this booklet and with a little help from friends, you can make your tub and have a hot bath all on the same day!! Your new tub will be a great conversation piece and a fun way to get to know your friends!! And it is guaranteed to inspire you to spend quality time outdoors with Mother Nature, relax your muscles and keep you clean!!

To create this simple low cost, low tech bath you will need a metal tub with a plug, some rocks, a small truck load of dirt, a bale of straw, a tarp, some firewood and something to make a stovepipe out of! And that's about it! The fire box for this project is made out of cob (a mixture of sand, clay and straw mushed together with water).

If you are just starting out on a piece of land, this tub will be a perfect beginning to making the land your "home".

MICHAEL'S COB HOUSE IN OREGON, BUILT IN 1994

Cob has been used for centuries to make long-lasting load-bearing buildings, garden walls, fireplaces and earthen ovens. And now hot tubs!! This project is ideal for acquainting yourself with cob building.

Your bath can be one of the main elements of a whole back yard creation. Imagine flowing cob courtyard walls and benches, wood/changing/garden shed, mosaics, gardens, fountains, gazebo...your outdoor dream home sweet home!! Read on!

PLANNING YOUR HOT TUB...

Read through this booklet to help you plan your tub. You may not be able to score 100% on all the considerations, but make thoughtful choices!

Things to consider

> the tub itself

> a dry place for your tub.

> a sensible place for the drain water to flow

> Where is the water for your bath coming from?

> stovepipe uphill of the fire

> Will you have a shed for changing and for firewood? Where will it be in relation to the bath?

> view from the bath

> wind

> privacy

> access to bath for wood, bathers, building materials

> design the tub area too

Read on for more details!

The tub itself

Just about any metal tub will do. In rich countries, remodelers rip them out of old houses and throw them away everyday.

The thinner the metal, the faster the fire heats the tub. Obviously the bigger the tub the more water and the more firewood and time it will take to heat it. Assess the amount of water and wood you will want to use and the number of people you want to share your bath with. To minimize burning wood, use a smaller tub made of thin metal. If you seriously need to conserve water where you live and still want a big tub, you can leave the same water in for 3 or 4 days if you add a cup of vinegar after bathing each day. This is good for your skin and hair and keeps the water fresh. For longer periods of time, you can use chemicals and a filter system like a regular hot tub. I have never done so myself but if you need more info about this, check with hot tub manufacturers.

THREE GALS IN A TUB

Photo by Pat Borowicz

Horse troughs

How many people do you want in your bath at once? If your philosophy is, more than one and/or if you like a deeper bath, I suggest a galvanized steel horse trough tub. In the USA these can be bought at your local farm and feed store. They are pretty reasonably priced. In 2001 in Oregon, USA, an 8 foot long metal tub costs $115. This will comfortably accommodate 5 people at once, two and a half feet deep. If you want a Japanese type furo for one person, you can get a 2 foot wide by 2 foot deep by 3 foot long horse trough for $50. One person can get completely immersed in it with their legs bent.

All the horse troughs I've ever met have a pathetic drain design which comes out the side so you can not drain the water completely when it's not in use and the tub gets yukky on the bottom. To prevent this, permanently plug the side drain. It's easy to do because it comes with a screw type plug. Drill another drain hole in the bottom of the tub and add a regular tub drain fitting and drain pipe like in this picture. Recycled metal drain parts are best because they last longer and you don't have to buy all that overflow stuff which most new ones come with. But if all you can find is the plastic ones, they'll work.

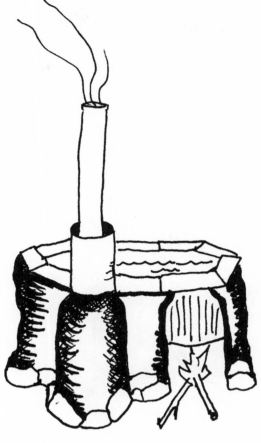

Round hot tubs

I have never tried it but I am sure it would work to use a round horse trough, or a cutdown old metal water or milk tank. To get the most out of the fire, make a spiral shaped firebox. To keep the draft going strong, make the firebox smaller as it gets further from the fire and closer to the chimney. You can do this by adding gravel or soil to the floor of the firebox and/or by making the central support partition off center.

Protect the drain from the fire by burying it in the cob of the central support column.

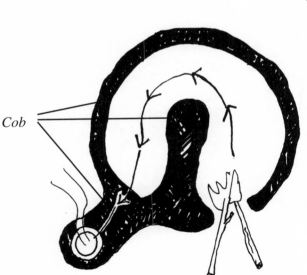

Cob

Birds eye view of fire/heat path under tub

After you have cut your tank down to size, you will need to smooth off the top lip or make a wooden seat around the tub.

If you live where horse troughs are available, you can buy great round ones.

Enameled steel baths

Household enameled steel bathtubs are great for a smaller bath. These are easy to get for free if you can intercept one on the way to the dump or the metal recyclers. They heat up much more quickly than the cast iron ones and are so much easier to transport to the site.

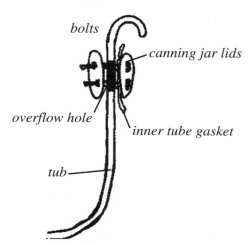

BLOCK OVERFLOW HOLE

bolts

canning jar lids

overflow hole

inner tube gasket

tub

For some unknown reason, regular bathtubs are almost always too shallow for adults to immerse themselves in! I suggest blocking off the overflow hole so you can fill the tub as full as possible. You can use an old inner tube for gasket material and two canning jar lids with a hole drilled through them bolted together to block off the overflow hole.

If you use a tub that has a false front on one side where the metal goes back down to meet the floor of a bathroom, you will need to make allowances for the drain. Either run the drain on the other side of the tub or out the end or rig up some way for the drain pipe to extend far enough below the tub to go under the false front.

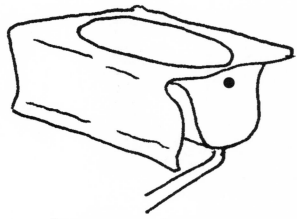

ENAMEL TUB WITH A FALSE FRONT

Cast iron tubs

We used to make all our outdoor tubs with these, thinking they were necessary to handle the fire but, not true. They take longer to heat up. They do come in bigger sizes than the enameled ones and they are easy to find for free. You'll need to block off the overflow hole to get maximum depth. (See page 10.) If this is what you have, use it! These old tubs are very heavy! Get lots of help and be careful while moving it. You can use long 2x4s to make a frame with handles so lot's of people can hold on and lift it at once. I have also moved the heavy tubs by rolling them on short sections of round pipes.

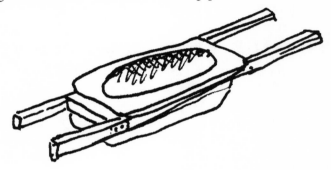

Wooden tubs

When I was a kid I lived in Hawaii and in our basement we had a Japanese furo. As my child's mind remembers it, the furo was made of 2 inch redwood boards screwed together with non-rusting screws and covered on the bottom with a copper sheet. I imagine variations on this theme would work. The redwood boards would swell with the water and seal the seams where the boards met. The copper bottom protected the wood from the fire. If any of you readers know anything about this, please let me know.

Choose a naturally dry place for your tub or create one.

Fires don't like wet. Make your tub somewhere that is naturally dry. A slight rise might be a good place or a little ridge between runoff places, or a rocky area. If you don't have a dryish spot then you'll have to make one by digging a drainage ditch uphill of where your tub will be, running around the tub and draining the water out of your way. Or you can build a pile of rocks or gravel for a dry base and make the foundation and tub on top of this.

Drain the tub to somewhere sensible.

Use the drain water for plants!! Run the water far enough away from the tub to keep the fire, firewood and walking areas as dry as possible.

Run the drainpipe to where you want the water. It's usually buried to protect it and to hide it. You can dig a hole or trench where the water leaves the drain pipe and fill it with pumice, cinders or river gravel. The further the gray water runs under the ground and through the gravel the cleaner it will become. Keep soaps to a minimum and buy biodegradable ones. Hot drain water can burn roots!! So if you are running the water directly to your garden or orchard, let it cool in the tub before running it out.

You can attach a flexible pipe to the end of the drain pipe so you can move the water to wherever you want it at the time. The absolute simplest drain system is to just dig a trench from under the tub drain to wherever you want it to flow and either leave it open or fill with gravel. And plant along it.

Where is the bath water coming from?

Think about where your water is coming from for your bath and put the pipes where they work for you. Obviously the closer to the water source the less hassle and cost there will be. You can connect the water source to the tub faucet or tap once the tub is built or you can just use a hose with a good shut off valve at it's end. If you decide to use a hose, you can eliminate or remove the faucets and make it more comfortable for two to sit in the tub and lean on either end.

How will the tub sit on the slope of the land?

The heat from the fire will naturally want to go uphill along the ground under the tub and into the stovepipe. This fact needs to be weighed with the other site choices. When you have positioned the tub, add gravel or dirt under it to make the base of the fire box level or ideally slanted upwards towards the stovepipe.

A raised fire is easier to tend so you can either put it on quite a steep slope with the fire facing down the hill or build up the whole tub with rocks and/or gravel and cob. Design it so the bathers have safe easy access in and out of the tub. Areas can be leveled and the dirt used to make cob.

Where does the firewood shed/bath house sit in relation to the tub?

A roof over a naturally dry area makes it easy to keep your firewood dry. It is not essential but you may want to think about how a bath/ firewood shed will fit with the tub so you can make one later. In the meantime, just cover the firewood pile with a tarp. If you do decide to build a shed, design it so you have easy access to deliver and fetch the firewood. You'll probably want to use it for dressing and undressing and for keeping towels and clothes dry in rainy or snowy weather.

Will you be collecting rain water for the bath or garden from the shed? If so, position it so you can gravity feed the water and make sure you have a good overflow system on the holding tank. Place the shed so that the water from the roof isn't running underneath the tub or the shed! This way the fire and the firewood stay dry. If possible, position the shed so the smoke from your tub fire won't blow into it. If the sun shines on the firewood, it will help dry it out. The shed can serve as a privacy screen but try not to block your views.

What do you want to look at when you're at repose in the tub?

Consider the positions bathers will sit in to see the views, the stars and the moon. Spend a little time observing the surroundings at the site. Where are the lights at night? Also think about the backdrop for yourself and your friends sitting around watching the fire and chatting with the bather(s). Position the tub so fire watchers can sit out of the smoke and on something relatively level. You may want to build benches later for seats.

Which way does the wind blow?

Align the smoke stack so the prevailing wind blows the smoke somewhere other than into the bathers faces or run the stovepipe high enough so the smoke blows above the people. Also think about what else is downwind. Keep the smoke from blowing into your house and changing shed! The most effective windbreaks have 40% airflow. A solid windbreak creates rotors and stronger winds behind it.

Privacy is nice while bathing.

Unless you are lucky enough to have a place where you don't need to concern yourself with such things, you will want to think about the line of sight from the driveway, the neighbors and the house. You can pick a place that's nestled away or protected from sight or you can create privacy by planting tall vegies, vines on a trellis of some kind, planting large bushes, or by building a more solid fence or cob wall. You can stack firewood like a fence for privacy, weave branches or brush, hang cloth between posts or position your woodshed to block the view or, just don't worry about it.

Get the tub, materials, water and firewood to the site.

You will need to get all the stuff to the site. (See materials list on pages 16-17) Obviously it is easier to drive everything to the site than to wheelbarrow it. Consider how much you will be carrying and from where and choose a site that works best for you. Where is the water coming from and how? Do you have enough water pressure to get the water to the site?

Design the area around the tub too.

A **wood shed/changing shed** is a practical addition to any outdoor tub. You might want to think about a good place for it when you decide where to put the bath. Think about the paths to the shed and around the bath.

It's very lovely to have **seating around the bath** area. People like to sit and chat with the bathers and they like to look at the fire so keep these things in mind as you design the tub. Put the fire so folks have room to sit and watch it.

A warm seat or towel warming spot can be made out of cob on top of the horizontal part of the stove pipe.

Any large **sculpture** needs to be built as you cob so design it and make the foundation to accommodate your art!

Other things to consider when choosing a site and designing your tub:

> deck for bare wet feet
> lighting
> places for clothes and towels
> cover or roof for bath
> landscaping and gardens
> paths in the area

MATERIALS LIST FOR YOUR HOT TUB:

for a basic tub:

> an old tub with a plug

> rocks

> dirt

> straw

> water

> firewood

> piece of wood for the inside on the bottom of the tub

> something to make a stove pipe out of, like rolled up roofing iron or coffee cans or you can make the whole pipe simply out of cob

> a tarp to mix the cob on and to keep tub covered when not in use

for a more "sophisticated" tub:

> a metal bathtub or horse trough

> drain attachments and a drain pipe long enough to get the drain water to where you want it.

> plug for the tub drain,

> plug for the overflow hole (optional)

> pumice, cinders or gravel for a mini drain field

> a water source and a faucet or hose with a good nozzle to turn it on & off at the tub

> two or three lengths of stovepipe (6 or 8 inch) and a stovepipe elbow (can be recycled) or something to make a stovepipe out of like a rolled up piece of metal roofing *spark arrester and rain cap (optional)

> a piece of insulated stovepipe or stuff to make your own double pipe system and a metal cap to keep the rain out from between the pipes   (See page 38 for more details)

> non-burning insulation (See page 38 for more details)

> rocks or broken concrete for a foundation

> 1 bale of straw, or lots of grass stalks

> sandy, clayey dirt or stuff to adjust your dirt to make cob (See section on cob starting on page 31)

> a pallet or some milled wood for a little deck for your feet when you get in and out

> a nearby tree or drift wood rack or elegant trellis for hanging towels and clothes

> firewood to heat the water

> two pieces of 3/4" or 1" x at least 10 inches board or a wooden rack for the bottom of the tub to protect your bottom and feet from the hot floor of the tub

> a dishpan for clean water to rinse off your feet before you get in

> wood for shelving around the tub (optional) See picture on page 41.

Tools:

SHOVEL
WHEELBARROW
TARP
LEVEL

REASONABLY STRAIGHT PIECE OF WOOD TO GO ACROSS TUB FOR LEVELING
BUCKET
HOSE (OFF/ON NOZZLE)
HATCHET &/OR CLEAVER

OK, TIME TO MAKE THE TUB!

Read this whole booklet and contemplate the pictures before you start! The more you understand it, the smoother things will flow. When you are designing and imagining your tub, do so **at the site** where it will be.

After deciding where the tub goes, get all the stuff and your tools together and get the water to the site. Make test bricks. (See page 33) Gather your friends to help! Have food and drinking water nearby! Keep this booklet handy as you build and reread it as you go! Set up the drain on the tub. And go for it!!

MAIN DIAGRAM OF WOOD-FIRED HOT TUB

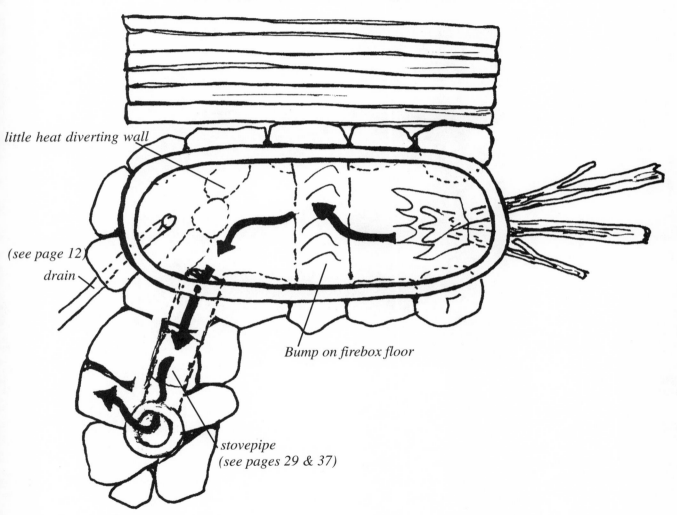

little heat diverting wall

(see page 12)

drain

Bump on firebox floor

stovepipe
(see pages 29 & 37)

The foundation
The whole idea

The fire will be flowing from the non-drain end of the bath along the tub, towards the drain and out the stove pipe on the side of the tub at the drain end. When building the foundation, it is easiest to build up 4 points with rock or concrete blocks to temporarily support the weight of the tub until the rest of the foundation is made and the cob has dried. The cob for the fire box sits on top of the foundation. The rocks make a base for the cob and keep it from touching the ground and wicking up moisture.

CONCRETE BLOCKS TO SUPPORT THE TUB WHILE BUILDING

You can use rocks, broken concrete pieces, concrete blocks or bricks for your foundation. They can be left showing or covered with cob and/or plaster depending on the look you want and what you have available. If you keep your eyes open, you will find foundation material either on your land, on the side of the road, at a building site or even in a dump. If you are really stuck for foundation material, you can even build the cob right on top of a pile of gravel. If the spot where you are making the tub might get wet, the gravel is a good idea whether you make a foundation or not. It will keep the fire area dry. You can raise the fire area up a little with foundation materials and gravel making the fire tending easier on your back. For this booklet I will use the words, 'rock' or 'stone' whenever I talk about foundations.

Temporarily set up all the pieces: the stovepipe, the drain and the tub with some rocks so you can see the overall picture and make sure everything is going to work with each other. Imagine possible future additions at this stage...the wood/changing shed, the benches, plants, deck, towel racks and any sculptures or arty bits.

Here's a check list:
> Stovepipe in place as close to drain as possible, with a little wall between them?
> Drain in place?
> Drainage area planned?
> Height of tub OK?
> Tub leveled side to side?
> Tub angled slightly down towards drain?
> Stovepipe rise far enough from tub?
> Enough rocks or foundation material?

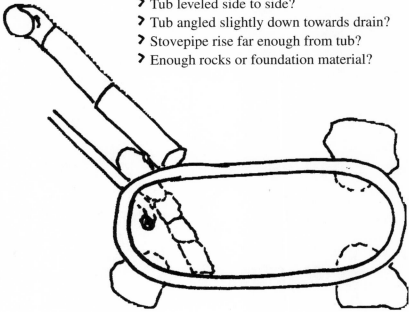

Starting your foundation

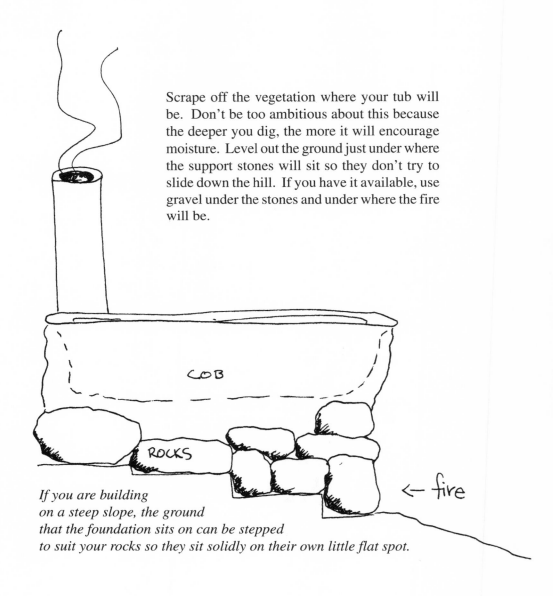

Scrape off the vegetation where your tub will be. Don't be too ambitious about this because the deeper you dig, the more it will encourage moisture. Level out the ground just under where the support stones will sit so they don't try to slide down the hill. If you have it available, use gravel under the stones and under where the fire will be.

COB

ROCKS

← fire

If you are building
on a steep slope, the ground
that the foundation sits on can be stepped
to suit your rocks so they sit solidly on their own little flat spot.

When you lay the initial support rocks begin at the non-drain end of the tub and get it **level from side to side** and establish the height you want. (See pages 25-26 for more details about height)

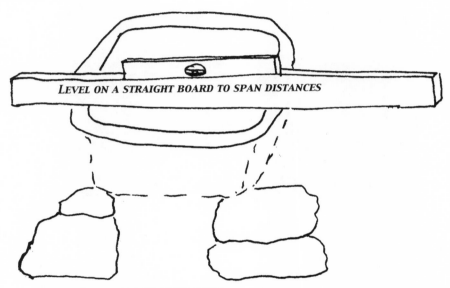

LEVEL ON A STRAIGHT BOARD TO SPAN DISTANCES

SET UP THE FIRE END FIRST.

Choose large stable rocks that set the tub at about the right height for these initial supports. You can add another smaller well chosen flat stone between the support rock and the tub, or between the support rock and the ground if necessary. If your rock is a little too high, you can dig down deeper into the ground to adjust the height. Put your most beautiful rocks at the fire entry as they (and the cob sitting on them) will frame the view of your fire.

Remember when choosing and positioning the main support rocks at the fire end of the tub that you will want to lay **a door** (a piece of sheet metal or roofing iron) **across the fire mouth** to control the amount of air to the fire. Think ahead to where the cob will be and use rocks that allow for a reasonably flat door opening. You can use a piece of something flat as a guide. Don't be too fussy about this.

A PIECE OF ROOFING IRON MAKES A GOOD FIRE DOOR

Then set up the support rocks at the drain end of the tub. Place them so this end of the tub is **slightly lower** than the fire end so the water will drain all the way out when you empty it. Keep them **out of the way of the drain system**. Set it up **so the stove pipe will fit** and be in the right position where it exits the firebox.

All this will take a bit of patience, reselecting and readjusting rocks, drain, stovepipe and tub position. This is a very important step and it is worth taking the time to make everything work together. If you are using a cast iron tub, make sure that it is very stable as it could really hurt someone if it falls.

The foundation needs to be **a couple of inches narrower than the bottom of the tub and about one foot wide**. Make a wider foundation for the bigger tubs and for where you plan to make sculptural design. If you are planning to make a cob bench or wall attached to the tub, you may want to at least start that part of the foundation as well, so it ties into the tub foundation.

Height of the tub off the ground

The fire end of the tub needs to be at least a foot off the ground for a fire to sit comfortably under it. A foot and a half is better. Next support the other end of the tub making sure that there is enough height for the drain pipe elbow and the stove pipe to exit the firebox. Remember to prop a piece of stove pipe where it goes with foundation stones to make sure you have enough height for it.

Make sure that the drain end of the bath is high enough to accommodate the drain pipe and the stove pipe and still have it lower than the other end, so water will empty out and drain completely. Otherwise the last bit of water sits in there and gets yukky. An easy way to check this is to pour some water in the tub and see if it empties.

THE DRAIN END NEEDS TO BE THE LOWEST POINT OF THE TUB.

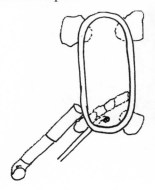

For the bigger tubs especially, I like to make the fire box high enough so the smallest, most unclaustrophobic builder can get into it and smooth the cob on the insides of the foundation and fire box. Making it this high allows for a big fast fire and gives easy access for removing the ashes, as well as making the building process easier. For the smaller tubs make the firebox high enough so you can stretch your shoulders and arms in under the tub to smooth the cob inside the fire box.

The process of getting the tub set up just right is very important and may need adjusting a few times. Take your time, read through this section again and use your brains and patience

SMOOTHING AND COMPACTING THE COB ON THE INSIDE OF THE FIREBOX SO THE FIRE WILL DRAW SMOOTHLY

The rest of the tub's foundation

When you have the tub sitting on rocks the way you want it, fill in between your supporting points on the long sides of the tub (not the ends) with stones for the cob to sit on. In general, it's best to make the foundation wider than you think you will want it. You only need enough foundation to keep the cob from touching the ground. Make your foundation so it will support any sculpture and tie into the foundation for benches you will want later.

Remember to put gravel under and between the rocks if you have some.

OVERLAP FOUNDATION ROCKS.

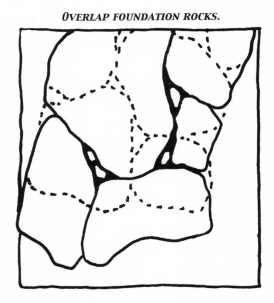

If you are doing more than one layer of foundation stones, place them like you would bricks so that each one spans the crack between the ones below it. Make sure every rock is stable and happy where it is. You can use little stone wedges and flat ones to make the big ones happy. The top surfaces of the stones need to support the cob that will sit on them so don't make the supporting rock surfaces too steep or the cob will tend to slip off. Also when placing the stones, look inside the fire box and think like fire. Set the stones so the fire can smoothly flow along the walls. You will only need one or two layers of rock, just enough to keep the cob off the ground.

Foundation for the drain end of tub

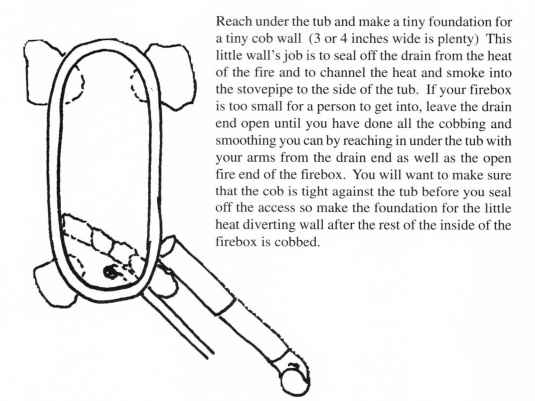

Reach under the tub and make a tiny foundation for a tiny cob wall (3 or 4 inches wide is plenty) This little wall's job is to seal off the drain from the heat of the fire and to channel the heat and smoke into the stovepipe to the side of the tub. If your firebox is too small for a person to get into, leave the drain end open until you have done all the cobbing and smoothing you can by reaching in under the tub with your arms from the drain end as well as the open fire end of the firebox. You will want to make sure that the cob is tight against the tub before you seal off the access so make the foundation for the little heat diverting wall after the rest of the inside of the firebox is cobbed.

It is optional whether you build a foundation and cob at the very end of the tub to cover the drain. It can be left open for easy access to any unfinished plumbing and for making sure the drain is not leaking but in the long term you will probably want to cob over it because cob is so much more beautiful than a drain pipe. You can always break away the cob, if for some unlikely reason you want to get to the drain and/or plumbing. The simplest drain system I have ever made was to just let the water pour out from the plug hole onto the ground and channel it with a little ditch into the nearby orchard. I used gravel on the ground and a lot of rock surrounding the drain area and minimal cob. It worked OK.

Foundation for the stove pipe

Fire and heat flow up. With the drain in place, use pieces of foundation to prop a length of stove pipe in place. You want the fire to flow along the bottom of the bath and be diverted side wards along the little wall protecting the drain, and gracefully out the side of the tub into the horizontal part of the stovepipe where it leaves the fire box under the tub. The stovepipe should be **resting against the bottom of the tub.** Put it somewhere near perpendicular to the length of the tub and **angle it slightly upwards towards the chimney**. You may want to add another piece of stove pipe at the other end before you put the elbow on it. This gets the hot pipe further away from the bathers. Remember to **make the foundation at the elbow wide enough to hold the cob** that is supporting the **chimney system** and the insulating pipe. (Read the section about insulating the stove pipe too! Page 38) In general **make the stovepipe foundation area bigger than you would think** necessary and use lots of rocks to save you cob. This area can become a warm bench for bottoms and towels.

PUT THE STOVEPIPE AGAINST THE BOTTOM OF THE TUB

A bump on the firebox floor

Some folks make a bump on the firebox floor to guide the fire onto the bottom of the tub. You can build this out of rocks and cob or just cob. Put it behind the fire under the middle of the tub in front of the drain protection wall. The purpose of the bump is to bounce the heat that is rushing to get up the stovepipe upwards onto the bottom of the tub to speed the heating process. Make this bump about a third of the overall height of the fire box. This bump is optional. (See the main diagram on page 19.)

Cob

Cob is a mixture of sand, clay, straw and water. Avoid top soil and silt if possible. A good mix for cob is about 3 parts sand to 1 part clay with straw added to taste. One part paper pulp to 10 parts cob is a yummy optional addition.

Your soil will be a combination of things. Use it as a base and add as little imported stuff as possible.

If you are interested in building larger structures out of cob, you will want to get *"The Cob Builder's Handbook, You Can Sculpt Your Own Home"* by Becky Bee, to learn more about structural cobbing and design. But for a tub, here's the quick version of how to make cob.

BILLIE'S COB HOUSE IN SOUTHERN OREGON 1995, SITE OF BECKY'S FIRST WORKSHOPS

SOIL TEST

Remove any stones or pebbles from a cup of soil that you want to test. Place soil into a quart jar. Then fill it 3/4 of the way with water, put the lid on and give it a **really good** shake. Then let it settle. The sand is heaviest and will fall to the bottom immediately as you watch. Next the silt will settle more slowly and the clay will stay suspended in the water for a while then settle on top of the silt. This simple test will give you a rough idea of what your soil is made of at the place where you collected the sample. Look at soil from different depths and different places. Soil can vary a lot in a small area.

Making test bricks

Read about how to make cob on the following page then mix up some samples of various soils from around your land. You can omit the straw for the testing. Form the mixtures into bricks or pies and label them well as to where they came from. Let them dry completely. To do so, place them on a grate or mat so air can get to the undersides. Once they've dried, analyze your results:

If your test bricks cracked, it means there's too much clay. If this happens, you'll need to add some sand. Make some new test bricks adding different amounts of sand. Again, remember to label them.

When your bricks are really dry try rubbing them with your thumbnail. If it's really **dusty and flaky, it means either too much silt or too much sand**. You will probably have an idea of which it is from the jar test. Add clay to your new test bricks if it's too sandy. Or both sand and clay if it's really silty.

The idea is to use as much clay as possible to make it strong while adding as much sand as it takes to prevent cracking. (Straw and paper pulp also help control cracking.)

I like to lightly (and as evenly as possible) spray water on the best test bricks with a hose and see which ones hold up the best. Then let them dry thoroughly again and try breaking them. Obviously the stronger the better.

Adjust your mix with a combination of your soils if necessary or bring in what you need and make new test bricks.

<u>Sand</u> Coarse sand with different sized particles is best. This can often be found along creeks and rivers. Buying concrete sand is cheap and easily available.

<u>Clay</u> Depending on the geology of where you live, you can probably find clay in a road cut or a washed out area. Like the jar test, when clay gets wet it settles on top and when it dries it cracks like those pictures of Death Valley. This can help you identify it. These cracked up chunks can be harvested for your cob mix. When dry it is very hard. If you have very pure clay, you will either need to crush it when dry or soak it and mush it into a clay slip that can be added to sand to make cob. You can also buy clay at a pottery supply place. Get the 50 pound bags of ball clay.

<u>Straw</u> Find straw (not hay) for your cob that's yellow and clean. Keep it dry until you are ready to use it because it will mold if it gets wet. If you are a real purist or if it's hard to come by straw where you are, you can collect grass stalks or fibrous plants to use in place of straw.

Making cob

Measure the soils that you have decided to use for your cob and put them onto a plastic or canvas tarp near where the tub will be. If you are mixing clay and sand, break up the chunks and stir the two together dry by rolling the tarp. Little stones are OK. Add water (a bit at a time so you don't get it too wet) and tromp on the dirt with your feet (bare ones work best) until everything is well mixed and the consistency of brownie dough. **Stir the mixture often** while tromping by lifting one edge of the tarp and pulling it towards you, bringing the stuff together into a roll. This speeds up the process and helps it mix thoroughly. Keep treading until the mixture holds together like a loaf when you roll the tarp. **Mixing the ingredients really well makes the cob strong!**

Then squish the mixture flat and sprinkle handfuls of straw lightly and evenly onto your brownie mix, roll that up like a cinnamon roll with the tarp then squish it all flat again. Do this about 3 times and mix the straw in well. When you grab a handful of cob it should look hairy with bits of straw sticking out between your fingers. Too much straw makes the mix crumbly. The cob should be like a dry cookie dough with straw in it. A little practice and your intuition will soon tell you the right amount of straw.

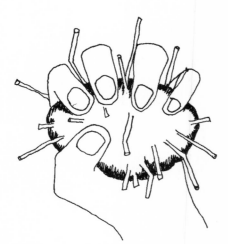

RIGHT AMOUNT OF STRAW

If the cob gets too dry, you can add more water. If it's too wet, add more straw or dry ingredients or let it sit and dry out a bit. With a little experimentation you'll learn to judge the moisture level just right. The cob should be similar to a dry cookie dough consistency, stiff enough to support it's own weight. If it's too wet and starts sagging when you are building with it, let it dry a little before adding more cob and make your next batch a little drier.

Building with cob

Lift blobs of cob to your foundation and mush it together with itself using your hands and a stick. Build onto your foundation up to the bottom of the tub. Push cob between the rocks on the outside for looks and on the inside of the firebox to make a smooth flow for the fire. You can cover the foundation too.

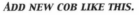

ADD NEW COB LIKE THIS.   **NOT LIKE THIS.**

Push the cob tight against the bottom of the tub and keep cobbing at least 1/2 way up the outside of the tub pushing it hard against the tub to prevent smoke seeping out. While the cob is still pliable keep an eye on it and push it back tight if it tries to slump away from the tub. **Smooth the cob inside the firebox and make sure it too is tight against the tub.** A good way to do this is to get one person (or hand) on the inside of the wall and one on the outside to push against each other and compact the cob against the bottom of the tub.

You can build the cob all the way up to the lip of the tub. This helps keep the water from cooling off too quickly and looks good.

Photo by Kyla   **ART BY KYLA AND JILL**

As you put the cob on, remember to take this opportunity to let your artistic talents show! Free your inspiration!! Cob is a very forgiving material and easy to change if you don't like something.

Unlike this photograph, I recommend putting the firebox opening at the end of the tub so the water heats more evenly and efficiently.

Build up under and around the stovepipe until it is well supported by the rocks and cob. Put up the insulating pipe too and stabilize it with cob. (See the next section about stovepipes for details)

Remember to build up the little wall to protect the drain and guide the heat into the stovepipe. (See page 28 to get the little wall in the right place.)

Unlike concrete, cob can be added to anytime. If you want to change something, or patch a crack or access plumbing, you can chip away what you don't want. Rewet the area well, make it rough and add cob.

18 FOOT LONG COB BENCH MADE AT THE MICHIGAN WOMEN'S FESTIVAL-BECKY BEE WORKSHOP 1998

Start your art from the bottom up. Make the foundation and the cob extra fat and let it ooge (bulge and sag) over the foundation so you can refine your sculptures by carving the extra cob away as the forms evolve. This can be done anytime but it's easiest before the cob hardens completely. An old hatchet and a cleaver are good cob carving tools.

You can add stones and cob as your design evolves while the cob is still wet.

The stove pipe

Used stove pipes are easy to find. In some parts of the "developed" world it seems that every other garage or shed has a piece of old stove pipe or two. Any part of the stove pipe or elbow that will be covered with cob can be holey and/or rusty. The pipe is really just a form for the cob. **Two three foot pieces running vertically from the elbow gives the fire on an outdoor bath enough draw.**

I've used old tin cans for forms, or old ceramic irrigation tiles. I've even just sculpted the flue by hand with no forms. Another way to make a stovepipe is to roll up a piece of corrugated roofing iron and put a wire around it to hold it.

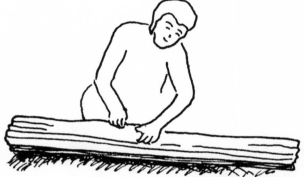

ROLL UP OLD CORRUGATED ROOFING IRON FOR A STOVE PIPE

To keep the draft operating properly, remember that the firebox and stove pipes should either stay the same dimension or get smaller as they get farther away from the fire. This will keep the draft flowing. Reducing the size of the passage increases the velocity of the heat.

Think about the wind direction when you place your stovepipe. No one likes smoke in their face!

Look up! When the heat leaves the chimney it is still hot enough to kill and possibly burn any foliage that is above and too close. If you live where forest or grass fires are a reality, you may opt for cold baths only during fire season. You can add a spark arrester (a 1/2 inchish screen) to the end of the chimney to decrease the fire danger. Use your best judgment on this!

Make sure that you build the stovepipe so no one in or out of the tub will accidentally touch it and burn themselves. Put it far enough away from the bather so if someone sits on the edge of the tub or the bench the hot pipe won't be touchable and/or insulate it well. (See next page.)

One way to protect people from the hot pipe is to build the cob up onto it high enough so folks won't get burned. If you cob up the pipe, make sure that the pipe is vertical. You can check it with a level. One option is to add as much pumice or perlite as you can to this cob to help insulate the pipe. The weather will slowly wear away any cob that is exposed but it can be replenished and replastered easily. Or you can put tiles or shingles over the cob to protect it from the rain.

For the fire to be as efficient as possible insulate the stovepipe with nonburnable insulation. This keeps the fire burning hot, therefore burning more thoroughly and producing less smoke. What I usually do is insulate the hot stove pipe with a double pipe system. Your tub will work fine with a single stove pipe cobbed over to prevent burns. The double pipe set up is really just a fancy optional extra but definitely worthwhile for indoor fires and tubs.

You can use a commercially made insulated pipe or make your own by adding a second larger pipe (outside one being at least 3 inches total larger than the inner stovepipe.) Then add non-burning insulation to the space between the two pipes. This includes wood ashes, pumice, vermiculite or perlite or any mixture of these. Make sure the insulation will not get wet in the rain by putting tiles over the cob or using a strip of sheet metal wrapped around the small pipe.

You can cob up the pipe far enough to hold it and the double insulating pipe securely then either leave the rest exposed to save making cob or cob all the way up for looks.

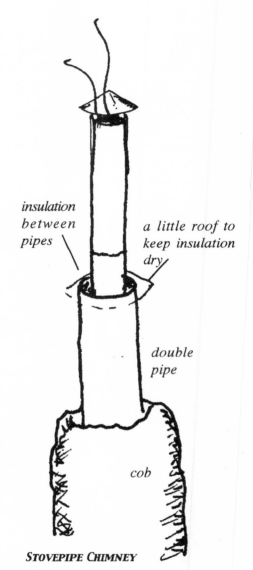

insulation between pipes

a little roof to keep insulation dry

double pipe

cob

STOVEPIPE CHIMNEY

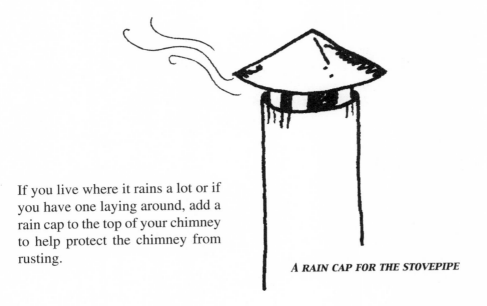

If you live where it rains a lot or if you have one laying around, add a rain cap to the top of your chimney to help protect the chimney from rusting.

A RAIN CAP FOR THE STOVEPIPE

If the tub is in a greenhouse or indoor bathroom, obviously you will need enough stove pipe to get the smoke out of the building. You can embed the stove pipe horizontally right into a cob wall. It is a good idea to insulate the stove pipe. To do so you can leave a 3 or 4 inch space as you sculpt the cob wall around the pipe and fill the space with non-burning insulation as you build. Or use a double pipe system filling between the pipes with insulation as with the outdoor baths as explained on the opposite page. An interior wall will hold the heat inside the house more efficiently than if it goes through an exterior wall. Make or buy an extra insulated double pipe system where the pipe meets the roof to prevent fires!

Decorating and protecting the cob from the weather

It is OK if the cob gets damp or wet occasionally. It only really needs protection during long wet periods and especially if it might freeze when it's wet. If it starts to erode, you can simply reapply some cob or plaster and it's just like new!

Here are some ideas for keeping your cob dry, extending it's life and making it more beautiful:

> Clay tiles or wooden shingles embedded in the top of the cob and overlapped like roof shingles makes a good little protective roof. We have used toilet tank tops for this and they work great too. If you have a tub with a lip on top, it's best if the tiles can sit tight up against the underside of the tubs lip, slanting slightly to guide the rain water away from the tub. As the cob is drying push it tight up under the tiles once or twice to hold them in place.

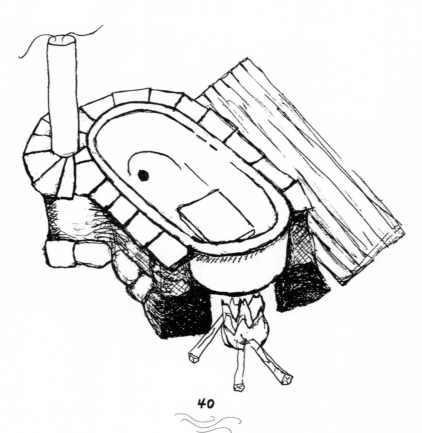

> Wide wood boards or planks are a great addition on the sides of the tub for seating and putting soap etc. They also serve as a little roof for the cob. To keep the tub cleaner, make sure that the runoff from these is flowing slightly away from, not into the tub. The shelf can be keyed into the cob by screwing smaller bits of wood onto the bottom of the shelf to be buried in the cob and thus held in place. You will need to **decide about having a shelf before you start to cob** so you can key it in well.

➤ A mixture of linseed oil (3 parts) and turpentine (1 part) painted onto the cob can be used to protect it from the elements. Some folks heat the mixture and add grated beeswax for added protection. This mixture is very flamable so be very careful if you do this!

➤ The simplest protection when the tub is not in use is a piece of roofing or plywood big enough to cover the cob on all sides of the tub. Weigh it or tie it down well so it doesn't blow off in the wind. This can also serve as a lid when heating the bath water.

Photo by Mitch Spiralstone

A SIMPLE PLYWOOD ROOF, MUST BE WEIGHED OR TIED DOWN!

➤ Put a roof over the tub area. A framework can be made over the tub so in the summer you can see the stars and in the winter it can be covered with a tarp or canvas, plywood or even plexiglass. Or put a permanent roof over the tub.

➤ Of course you can build the tub indoors, running the smoke out through a wall or through the roof like an ordinary stovepipe system. A tub is a wonderful and useful addition to a greenhouse, providing heat and moisture. As with any greenhouse, ventilation is essential.

Protecting the cob with plaster

ART BY MITCH & KIMBER & FRIENDS

Photo by Mitch Spiralstone

❯ Plastering the cob will help protect it from the weather and can be redone anytime. If you want to make your tub smooth and fancy looking, you can make a finer sifted version of the cob and smooth it on your cob creation like frosting. It's a good idea to make up some test batches. Put them on the cob and let them dry so you can choose the recipe you like the best. Like the cob, if it cracks when it dries add more fiber or sand and put on another layer or just don't worry about the cracks.

I usually use fresh cow or dry grated horse manure (Any grass eating animals poo will do.) in place of the straw as it is already " sifted and chopped" It seems to have a magic waterproofing effect too. If the dung is dry, sift it through a 1/2 inch mesh screen. Cow shit is smelly but easy to use and makes a fabulous plaster when it's fresh out of the cow. The smell will go away completely. You can use paper pulp instead or as well as the manure. Soak any kind of paper and pulp it. After reweting the cob, smear the frosting on the cob and when it is 1/2 dry you can polish it with a yogurt container lid (with rough edges cut off) or with a smooth rock. You can use different colored clays to make beautiful decorative plaster "paintings" on the cob.

The plaster can be sculpted into patterns and designs. You can push tiles or broken pottery or shells into the plaster for decorations. The paper pulp makes things stick well or you can add a little water based glue to the plaster under the decorations.

Beautifying your bathing area

Make a deck to step out of the bath onto! A wooden one is best for keeping feet warm and clean. Depending on the height of your tub, you may want to make a step between the tub and the deck. Some folks make stone or brick floors and steps around the tub.

Make beautiful driftwood towel and clothes racks or hang stuff on nearby trees.

Create your privacy screen if necessary. This can be a wall of woven sticks, cob or any ordinary fence. It can be a piece of canvas or material. A big stack of firewood or the firewood shed itself works. A trellis planted with climbing things or freestanding dense vegetation makes a lovely screen. This can be watered with the bath water.

Plant scented plants like jasmine, roses, bulbs, queen of the night, rosemary and lavender by the bath to scent the air and to use as romantic additions to the bath water.

Candles or lanterns at night are lovely. Alcoves can be built for them into the cob as it won't catch on fire. Or they can be hung from trees or use your imagination. A string of Christmas lights makes soft festive light.

A BEAUTIFUL COB KIOSK AT LOST VALLEY CENTER, OREGON BY BEE BECKY BEE & FRIENDS AT A WORKSHOP

The bath can be part of a whole artistic courtyard type outdoor living area with seating, a bath/firewood shed, gardens, walls, patios, roofs, mosaics, barbecue, cob oven and fountain. Dream it into being!! This is a wonderful way to claim an urban backyard and extend ones living space. Cob walls create dense privacy. They are great sound barriers as well as being beautiful to look at. Remember though that cob will need some protection from the elements. You can put little roofs on the walls and create simple low cost roofing over benches and your other cob creations. If you live where it's dry, you can leave the cob exposed with a good plaster or linseed oil finish. You may want to get our handbook for more information on cob building. See page 54.

THE ART OF USING A WOOD FIRED TUB!

As soon as you are finished cobbing you can fill the tub, make a fire and have a hot bath!! Hallelujah!! If you see any smoke escaping, push the cob tight while it is still soft to block off the leak. Because the cob is wet this first firing will take a little longer than the future ones. If you haven't built a deck to step out of the bath onto yet, you can use spare straw on the ground to keep your feet from getting dirty in the meantime.

Unless you have set up a tap on the tub, it's helpful to have a good non-leaking on-off switch on the tub end of your hose.

For everyday use, fill the tub in the morning if the air is warmer than the water so it can take the chill off and start the process of heating the water. This will save time and wood. Put the right amount of water in so when you get in it won't overflow. Don't walk away and leave the hose running because you might forget it!

You can cover the tub with clear plastic or plexiglass which might help the solar process to heat the water. If the days are hot, it's nice to dip into the cool water in the afternoon before you light the fire. If you live where the air is really hot part of the year, just use the tub for cool baths during that time. Cover the tub if you have a dog who likes to swim and to keep thirsty creatures, children and bugs out.

Firing up the tub

Of course, dry seasoned wood on hand makes fire building much easier and less smoky! You can collect long branches and limbs and feed them in as they burn to save yourself cutting the wood.

Make sure the tub has water in it before you start the fire. Get a plug that fits your drain hole really well. Beware of faulty plugs. As I learned the hard way, if the water is being pumped directly from a well and the hose is left in the tub the water can siphon itself back down into the well. That's how I discovered that a fire under an empty porcelain or enamel tub will crack the finish off. It was ugly but still worked fine. But please learn from my mistake!

Just like a pot while you are cooking **a lid on the tub speeds up the heating** time. A piece of plywood or old door works fine. I have also used those little foam camping mattresses cut to the size of the top of the water in the tub.

After you've started the fire, you can lay the fire door (a piece of tin works well) across the opening or part way across to control the amount of draft to the fire. With a little experimentation you will soon become a pro! A healthy fire takes about an hour to heat the water in a regular 5 foot cast iron tub, or a 4 person horse trough, less in a regular sized thinner steel enamel tub. The speed depends on the thickness of the tub, the dryness and quality of the wood, your fire making abilities, the water temperature and the air temperature. This is a great opportunity to sit and relax and stare at the fire. It can be a social happy hour time with lawn chairs (or cob benches), refreshments and friends.

If only one person is going to have a bath, you can let the fire go out or almost go out once the water is hot enough. If more than one person is bathing or if you want to stay in a hot bath for a long time, or if you like to increase the heat as you get used to it, you'll want to keep the coals hot enough to restart by adding another stick or two.

With a little practice you will get very good at estimating the right amount of fire for the temperature you like. At first it is easy to overheat the water. Be careful, especially with kids and folks who are differently abled! Remember that hands can handle hotter temperatures better than the rest of the body! Test the temperature with your elbow. If it gets a little too hot, you can get in butt first as butts handle heat better than feet. The feet can dangle over the edge until they get used to it. You can always add cold water if it gets too hot.

Another approach is to half fill the tub, heat that water really hot and add cold to adjust the temperature.

Hot seat!

The bottom of the tub gets too hot to be comfortable. You'll need two pieces of wood, one to sit on and one for your feet. (The sides of the bath are OK thanks to the cob.) Keep experimenting with different types of wood until you find a type that works well. Redwood or cedar are good. Avoid plywood or other glued or treated wood. Another option is to build a wooden grid for the bottom of the tub. Whatever you use, make it as thin as possible otherwise it raises the bather and makes for a shallower bath. To extend the life of the wood keep it out of the sun when not using it.

Another piece of wood that sits width wise across the top of the tub can be good for sitting on if you get too hot and for scrubbies, washcloths, candles etc.

Sharing the bath with friends

If you plan to share the bath water with a few friends, you can overfill the bath, heat it up and then have buckets of hot water for people to rinse off with before they get in. This is a good way of keeping the bath water cleaner and free of soap scum. Rinse off your feet before you get in. **A dishpan of water at the tubs edge encourages this practice.**

Usually the fire builder has first option for the bath or has the right to give the first bath to whoever they want. You can work out who goes next. It's interesting to note the bath order hierarchy. More than one good friend can fit quite well in a regular sized bathtub so try two at a time. I have heard of 5 people squeezed into a tub for fun but when they got out there was hardly any water left so consider this before you overflow the water in case there are more single bathers waiting. Speaking of overflowing, it's best to let the extra water out the drain so it doesn't overflow and wet the cob or the fire unless you already have set up the tub overflow as you would in any bathroom.

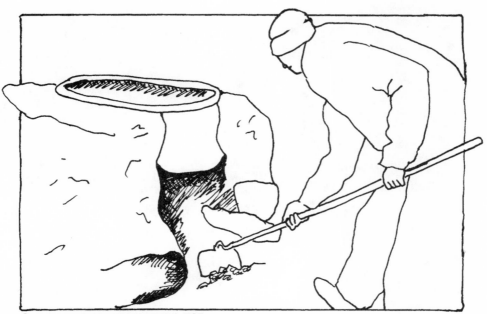

CLEAN OUT THE ASHES WITH A HOE

It might be more relaxing for later bathers to do so in the dark when they can't see how dirty the water is. Or you can always let out the dirty water and refill the tub and stoke up the fire. If you do this while the fire is still going, run the **hose onto the bottom of the tub between emptying and filling so it doesn't overheat** and crack up. I've been bathing like this off and on for decades and so far am as healthy as can be. When everyone is done you can throw in the dirty laundry to soak or bathe the dog or clean off the ring around the tub while the water is still hot and let the water out. Make sure the fire is out before you empty the tub.

Relax! Warm your Bones!
Get to Know the Sky!

ENJOY YOURSELF!

Well dear reader, I hope this book has taken you on a wonderful adventure and that a hot tub sits steaming nearby, ready for you and your loved ones to get into. May it give you pleasure and time and remind you of who you are!! Many blessings from the author and friends.

BILLIE'S COB HOUSE INSIDE, SOUTHERN OREGON 1995, VIEW OF OUTSIDE ON PAGE 31

Cob has been used for centuries to make long-lasting load-bearing buildings, garden walls, fireplaces and earthen ovens. Here are a few photographs to show you what some folks have created with cob! If you want more in depth information about how to create cob buildings, and apply earth plasters, get hold of *"The Cob Builders Handbook, You Can Hand Sculpt Your Own Home,"* by Becky Bee. Send $23.95 US to Becky Bee at **GROUNDWORKS, PO Box 381 Murphy, OR 97533.** Check out the web site at **http://www.beckybee.net**

SUNRAY'S STRAWBALE HOUSE WITH COB PLASTER, FLOORS, FIREPLACE AND FURNITURE

Cob can be used in conjunction with other building materials like Sunray did on this house. It's also great for making sculptured art forms, benches, alcoves, shelves, additions and renovations. Cob saves money and gives a lovely earthy feel to any house.

For more info or to order

"The Cob Builders Handbook, You Can Hand Sculpt Your Own Home" by Becky Bee

Photo by Jean King

Contact: **GROUNDWORKS**

PO Box 381 Murphy, OR 97533   **541-471-3470**

cob@beckybee.net

www.beckybee.net